Shot-Put

THE VIKING LIBRARY OF SPORTS SKILLS

SHOT-PUT

DR. FRANK RYAN

NEW YORK / THE VIKING PRESS

First published in 1973 by The Viking Press, Inc.
625 Madison Avenue, New York, N.Y. 10022

Published simultaneously in Canada by
The Macmillan Company of Canada Limited

SBN 670-64286-x

Library of Congress catalog card number: 72-75753

Printed in U.S.A.

Preface

We really don't know much about the early history of putting the shot. That story is lost in time. It does seem, however, that whenever primitive man was able to take some time out from eating and not being eaten, he indulged his rudimentary tendencies toward cultural activities, including sports and games. Sports activities were not completely divorced from everyday primitive strivings. Rather, sports were a light-hearted extension of these strivings. Running, jumping, and throwing had survival value. These basic activities became the foundation of games and sports—and they continue to be. It's difficult to think of a modern game that doesn't include one or more of these activities.

It would be a good guess that the shot-put, old as it is, came along later than some other sports. Although it does involve a kind of throw, the shot-put does not place much premium on accuracy. The primitive who threw at something—an enemy, subhuman or human—had to have a reasonable chance of hitting it. Therefore, it seems likely that the evolution of the shot-put as a game activity would not have occurred until mankind had a little more leisure. It probably became a contest of masculine strength in which the strong men of the tribe or village competed to see who could drive a heavy weight the farthest.

A clue to the history of a sporting event is often the measurement system used in it. For example, the weight of the discus and the diameter of the discus circle are specified evenly in the metric system. In contrast, the weight of the shot and the diameter of the circle from which it is thrown are specified in pounds and feet. Thus, we look to the continent of Europe for its influence on the discus throw, and we look to the British Isles for their influence on the development of the shot-put. Actually, the early event in the British Isles was called "putting the stone," and even today it is called "putting the weight." The stone weighs 14 pounds and is the origin of a measurement still in use: if you step on a scale in England or Ireland you read your weight in stones, or units of 14 pounds.

In the first modern Olympic Games, held at Athens in 1896, R. S. Garrett of the U.S.A. won the shot-put with a put of 36 feet, 2 inches. Shortly afterward, 40 feet was exceeded. In the early part of this century a giant of a man, Ralph Rose, astonished the world with a put of more than 51 feet. The experts pronounced this record unbeatable, and it did last a long time. It was inevitably broken; but even up to the Olympic Games of 1932, won by Leo Sexton with a new Olympic record of 52 feet, 6³⁄₁₆ inches, no one had bettered 53 feet.

After the 1932 Olympics there were some exciting duels between John Lyman of Stanford University and Jack Torrance of Louisiana State University. Torrance went over 53 feet. Lyman set a record at better than 54 feet. At the national championships Torrance defeated Lyman with a put of over 55 feet. In the summer of 1934, while on a European tour, Torrance got off a put of 57 feet, 1 inch. Before this great performance he had not reached the intermediate distance of 56 feet, and he never again did as much as 55 feet.

Torrance's record was hailed as a "perfect" one, a record that could never be broken. It looked that way. It wasn't until four years later that even a distance of 52 feet was exceeded in the U.S. national championships. But just prior to World War II there emerged a number of fine athletes who began to creep up on the "perfect" record. Among them was a well-coordinated giant, Al Blozis of Georgetown University, who bettered 56 feet a number of times.

In 1948 on a spring day at the Kansas Relays the athletic world was electrified by a report that a 58-foot put had been made. The "perfect" record had been broken. It was accomplished by Chuck Fonville of the University of Michigan. Fonville was not a massive giant and so did not fit the stereotype of a shot-putter, but he was a highly talented athlete with the ability to perform well in other events. Curiously, Chuck never reached 57 feet on his way to the world record.

A year before Fonville made his record, Jim Fuchs turned out for track at Yale University. In high school he had been an all-time great football player and a record-holding sprinter. At that time I was a young coach in charge of the field events at Yale. Fuchs was instantly recognized as a remarkable combination of speed and strength, and his progress was rapid. At the end of his sophomore year he was a member of the U.S. Olympic Team. The next year, 1950, he broke the world record for shot-put and went on to dominate this event completely. Jim Fuchs was the first shot-putter to break the world record routinely. Each previous record holder had made his one big put, but Jim would go over the official record several times in a single meet. He had the potential for a "big one" of surely well over 60 feet. There is no telling how far Jim might have put, but instead he moved along to his present career as a highly successful executive.

As Jim's coach, I was probably helpful in emphasizing the back position and long acceleration of the shot that would be needed for the next world record. But the precise method of getting this long drive evolved from Jim's ingenuity and ability.

On the West Coast of the United States a talented young giant, Parry O'Brien, was keeping an intelligent and ambitious eye on what was happening in shot-putting. Having observed Fuchs's technique, Parry was convinced that a long drive on the shot was a must. It was necessary to reach a power position with the trunk inclined toward the rear of the circle. Fuchs had done it, but his method was difficult to imitate. After thinking and experimenting, Parry O'Brien hit upon a different method of reaching the power position. Parry's invention left an indelible stamp on all shot-putting. His technique, currently used by all outstanding shot-putters, is called the "O'Brien Technique." It should be.

Parry O'Brien did invent an effective technique, but he should be thanked for more than that. He demonstrated the fantastic effects of weight training, and did much to break down the prejudices that coaches and athletes then held about this method of training. Parry also showed the value of intensive workouts. When Parry came East for the indoor meets, he often stayed with us at Yale. His practice sessions were long and hard. It was eye-opening and helpful to our squad members to see what a real workout looked like.

Parry became the first 59-footer, the first 60-footer, the first 61-footer, the first 62-footer, and the first 63-footer. For a long time he stood completely alone. There wasn't a real challenger in sight. In 1952 Parry established a new Olympic record—57 feet, 1.43 inches. He won again in 1956, this time bettering his own Olympic record by almost four feet. At the 1960 Olympic Games, held at Rome, Parry's performance was about two feet better than his Olympic record of 1956. But this time he had to settle for the silver medal instead of the gold. The championship was won by Bill Nieder, who shortly before the Games set a world record of 65 feet, 10 inches.

During the next four years Parry continued to compete and improve. In 1964 he made his fourth Olympic Team. At Tokyo he got off his best Olympic put ever. But there was no medal. Parry was fourth. The Olympic champ was Dallas Long, who had previously set a world record of 67 feet, 10 inches. The runner-up, destined to be the world record holder and next Olympic champion, was the incredible Randy Matson. Randy went on to set the current world record of 71 feet, 5¼ inches, a mark that defies belief.

As in the past, the experts have rushed in. They consider Randy Matson's record to be unbreakable. It could be so, for at the present writing, only Randy has done better than 71 feet. But a few others have done 70 feet. They seem to be knocking at the door.

About you. Why put the shot? Simply because it's fun. It's an enjoyable experience. You can ask the question "Why do it?" about any sports activity—golf, football, tennis, or swimming. Social scientists may think of deep-rooted psychological reasons for sports participation, but such participation is also enjoyable and satisfying. Educators cite such benefits as character and personality development. They are probably right, but participation in a sport works out best when you simply enjoy what you are doing.

We've just talked a little about the history of shot-putting. And it seems that each record holder was a bright, talented, and dedicated person. The question naturally arises "How can I compete with these gifted greats?" It's hard to tell. Someone is going to do it. It could be you. But even if the mathematical odds against enormous success seem great, you still can enjoy personal enrichment and fun along the way. It's best to keep the right combination of enormous hope and day-to-day enjoyment. If the hope is not actually realized, the enjoyment of the activity still can be there. Let's look at a simple example. In baseball Babe Ruth hit more than 700 home runs. No one has ever come close to this record, and if we take a hard look, it doesn't seem likely that anyone will. Yet, millions of young people play baseball. Some of the players may have fantasies of exceeding Ruth's records, but all of them can enjoy playing.

As for the shot-put, its basic simplicity may be part of its fascination. You have a round, fairly heavy object, and the task is to put it as far as you can. Man has always been intrigued by tests of strength, skill, and agility. What could be more basic than picking up a heavy object and seeing how far you can move it? You know that strength is going to be important, in addition to agility and technique. To do your best, you will want to develop all three factors.

When you first put the shot and before you compete with anyone else, you compete with yourself—perhaps in a sense you always do. You know your performance of yesterday or a week ago. And you can think today you'll do better. Competition against other athletes brings even more enjoyment. You'll have dual meets, town meets, country meets, and, as you progress, state meets. When your name is called in each competition, you will be alone in the circle. What you do will be up to you. If things go badly, there is always another day at the practice field, where you can improve your technique. And if things go well in competition, you will feel elated and look ahead to even better performances.

Contents

Shot-Put

Facilities, Equipment, and Rules

The shot-put is a very basic event and, accordingly, the facilities, equipment, and rules are extremely simple.

Facilities. When you first start, your basic needs are a level and firm surface of about 7 feet from which to operate and a place for the shot to land. Eventually, you will want an arc-shaped piece of wood to use as a toeboard. In formal competition the rules specify a circle 7 feet in diameter and a stop or toeboard at the front of the circle. The toeboard is made of wood and is in the shape of an arc so that the inner edge coincides with the edge of the circle. Along its inside the board measures 4 feet. It is 4 inches high and 4½ inches wide. The board is firmly fixed in place.

Some years ago shot-put circles were usually made of clay or cinders. The surfaces varied a great deal depending on their exact composition, maintenance, and the weather. The introduction of all-weather surfaces has brought dependability. Most circles now are of brushed cement. Facilities, since they are so simple, need not be much of a problem. If you are out for your school's track, a cement circle is probably already available. If not, it won't take long to put one down. A toeboard can be made quickly in the carpenter shop.

Equipment. You need the athletic clothing, including a warm sweat suit that is usually worn by all trackmen. In addition, you'll need one or more pairs of rubber-soled shoes. It could be useful to have a pair of spiked shoes in case you run into surfaces other than all-weather. Unlike the spikes worn by runners, yours should have heel spikes. Interchangeable spikes are best, so that you can adjust spike length to the surface conditions.

The shot itself is an inexpensive and durable piece of equipment. A shot can be made of almost any kind of metal, but iron is the cheapest and best. The surface of the shot should be slightly rough to prevent slipping.

If during the bad weather months you must practice in a gym or other indoor facility, get an indoor shot. The original indoor shots were of leather and stuffed with buckshot. The new plastic-covered indoor shots are superior, particularly because they can land on almost any surface without injuring it.

Rules. As in other sports, the purpose of the rules is to give everyone a fair shake, to have everyone compete under the same conditions. The rules for the shot-put are extremely simple. The basic rule is that you have to stay within the 7-foot circle. You can hang over the circle in any direction, but no part of your body can touch outside of it. The inside of the toeboard can be touched, as it surely is by all good shot-putters, but you cannot touch the top of the board. A fairly recent rule requires that you leave via the rear half of the circle.

The shot cannot "be brought behind the shoulder." But if you are making a normal put, this rule really doesn't make much difference. In many sports the rules can be highly complicated, and you have to be constantly aware of possible violations. But in shot-putting the rules are hardly restricting at all.

Over-all View

As a shot-putter your over-all goal is clear. You want to put the shot as far as possible and yet stay within the simple rules of the event. The physical setting for your efforts is a 7-foot circle with a toeboard at its front. Within this framework you try to perform as efficiently as possible.

For any given trajectory or angle of shot release, the distance the shot will travel from the athlete's hand to the landing spot will depend upon the speed at which the shot is moving when it leaves. Hence, practice efforts are directed toward creating shot velocity. In practice sessions these efforts take three forms: (1) improvement of technique, (2) building greater strength, and (3) developing more speed. These are the three areas that we will be talking about.

The best technique or form is simply the best way of using your muscles to drive the shot. As soon as possible in your career you should understand the various details of form. You will learn a point of form much more quickly and with more enthusiasm when you are convinced of the importance of that point and know in what way it makes a contribution to performance.

In this section we have photographic action sequences of three of the all-time greats of shot-putting—Parry O'Brien, Randy Matson, and Dallas Long. Each in turn was the world record holder and Olympic champion. Later on, when we get to some critical points of form, we will be reproducing some of these photos. Also, we will be looking at pictures of some shot-putters who seem to be on their way to greatness. In addition, we will be seeing photos of a beginner working with his coach.

5

These pictures will give us a better feel for the practical problems of getting started.

The action sequences of the greats are yours for constant reference. As you would expect, these athletes show excellence of form, and more and more you will perceive the common threads or denominators in what they do. Keep checking back to them.

Gross action. When we first look at the shot-put, the action seems pretty much as follows: The athlete starts at the rear of the circle, swings his left leg, drives across the circle, lands, and puts the shot. As we look a little closer, we can see more details. The position at the rear of the circle is one of balance and readiness. The legs coordinate to produce a smooth flow of action. Landing in the front part of the circle is stable with the upper part of the body inclined toward the rear. Drive against the shot is continuous and powerful. At the finish, body weight is balanced over the right leg. So we begin to distinguish several important parts of the event—a starting position, a glide across the circle, a solid landing position, a powerful drive, and a long follow-through.

Shot-put action looks simple, as it should, because simplicity and naturalness are needed for great performance. But this appearance of simplicity is somewhat deceptive. Shot-putting is a highly skilled act. The smoothness of movement is the result of understanding the event and countless hours of practice. One of the fascinating things about the shot-put is that it is composed of certain natural movements, while at the same time these movements are used within a framework that permits effective application of power.

Our approach. In learning the shot-put we will combine the practical approach with the theoretical. We want to learn the features that have proved valuable, those that have actually worked for the champs. But, at the same time, it is important to understand why they work.

Although shot-put action is continuous, it is useful as a learning procedure to regard the event as having two major divisions. These two divisions are (1) the power position at the front of the circle along with the drive made from this position and (2) the glide that brings you across the circle and into the power position with momentum. Hence, two of the larger sections of this book will be devoted to the "standing put" and "across the circle."

As a shot-putter progresses in his career, he is bound to meet the same problems and situations the greats have encountered along the way.

By taking advantage of their day-to-day experiences he can both speed up and improve the learning process.

For the sake of economy in using words we will assume you are right-handed. However, there is, of course, no reason a "lefty" cannot perform as well as a "righty." So if you happen to be left-handed, just reverse the words *right* and *left*.

1. Parry O'Brien left an indelible stamp on shot-putting. He broke the world record many times, won two Olympic championships, and was a member of four Olympic teams. He is immortalized for having invented the style that bears his name. The "O'Brien Technique" is used by every outstanding shot-putter in the world.

1a

1e

1f

1g

1k

1l

1m

1b

1c

1d

1h

1i

1j

1n

1o   1p

2a

2. Randy Matson, the greatest shot-putter of all time, shows the superb form that brought him an Olympic championship and made him the world's first seventy-footer.

2d

2e

2f

2j

2k

2l

2m

2b

2c

2g

2h

2i

2n

2o

2p

3a

3b

3. Dallas Long smashed the scholastic record by several feet and then went on to live up to his great promise. He became the world record holder and Olympic champion.

3c

3d

3e

3f

3g

Weight of the Shot

Shots of three different weights are used in competition. An 8-pound shot is used in junior high school and in competition for women. The senior high school athlete puts a 12-pound shot. In collegiate, national, and international competition, including the Olympic Games, the shot weighs 16 pounds. In competition, you will have to put whatever weight shot is required, but in practice sessions you can decide on the weight of the shot that you will use. Let's take a look at what the weight of a shot means for carrying out form.

Regardless of the weight of the shot certain fundamentals apply. Try to imagine yourself putting a 1-pound shot and then a 100-pound shot. In both cases you would do some things the same way. For example, you would want to be well balanced, and you would want to get a long acceleration of the shot. Yet there would be a difference in technique and great differences in timing. Looking at the topic of shot weight another way, suppose that the international and intercollegiate rules were changed so that the weight of the shot rose from 16 to 25 pounds. Techniques and timing would have to change. The same would be true if the weight was reduced from 16 pounds to, let's say, 10.

The introduction of weight-training methods has permitted shot-putters to develop enormous strength. They would be better just for being stronger. But there is a more important point. Their greatly increased strength has allowed modern shot-putters to change techniques and timing. Randy Matson, for example, although gifted with great natural strength, has had the advantage of weight training. To him a 16-pound shot may feel as heavy as an 8-pound shot felt to a fine performer of a generation ago.

For this reason Randy can do things the old performer could not do in his day.

Any particular shot has an objective weight as shown by the scales. Yet the subjective weight of the shot varies with the strength of the athlete. How heavy the shot is for *you* makes a difference in the form you can carry out. Even at an early stage you might be able to carry out a reasonably good imitation of Randy Matson's form while using a 6- or 8-pound shot. But you wouldn't be able to imitate Randy if you used a 16-pound shot.

Ideally, the weight of your shot and your physical strength should increase together. In order to get yourself ready to use the most effective form it's helpful to try to look ahead to what your future strength is going to be. You should start with a very light shot and then gradually increase the weight of the shot as you grow stronger. As you progress, the shot should never feel so heavy that it interferes with your ability to carry out form. You should always feel you can "whip" the shot. The shot should always be light enough for you to carry out any body movements you want to.

Just for the purpose of illustrating this one important point, let's take an ideal and impractical situation. Let's say there is only one goal—eventually winning the Olympic championship. At this starting point we want at least a rough measure of your strength. Weight lifting is a good measure of strength, although it is not a completely accurate one. Technique affects performance. Nevertheless, let's assume you can now press 100 pounds. Looking ahead two Olympiads, we estimate you will then be able to press 400 pounds. You would equate a press of 400 pounds with the ability to put a 16-pound shot. That means that your present press of 100 pounds would indicate the use of a shot weighing about 4 pounds. As your ability to press increased, you would increase the weight of the shot. When your press climbed to 200 pounds, the shot would weigh 8 pounds. By the time you press 300 pounds you would get to a 12-pound shot. You would use a 16-pound shot only when you have the ability to press 400 pounds.

The above illustration is impractical. Very few shot-putters have ever pressed 400 pounds. Also, a shot-putter has various levels of imminent competition during his career, and he has the practical problem of getting ready for each of them. Yet the general point still holds.

A shot of any given weight will be subjectively different for you as you become stronger. It's best to start with a light shot that is comfortable for you and to increase the weight of the shot as you gain strength. There is never a good reason to practice with a shot heavier than the one you will use in competition.

Shot-putters who work in practice with heavier-than-competition shots cite two "benefits." They say if you practice with an overweight shot, the standard shot feels lighter. It does feel lighter, but it doesn't go as far as it otherwise would. The second "benefit" cited is that the heavy shot builds strength. It does to a certain extent, but it builds strength at the expense of timing and technique. There are other, more effective ways of building strength, notably weight training, and these methods don't interfere with the execution of the event. A valuable general rule is to keep your strength-building efforts separate from your performance of the event.

Strength and Conditioning

The introduction of weight training has been the most significant factor in creating the record explosion that has taken place in the shot-put. All fine shot-putters are weight trainers. It's difficult to know exactly how much footage a good weight-training program adds to a shot-putter's performance, but 10 feet would probably be a conservative guess. An athlete who puts 60 feet would probably be putting 50 feet or less without the benefit of weight training.

If you want to be a good shot-putter, you really don't have a problem deciding whether or not you will weight train. Competitive performance simply requires weight training. After all, form and technique depend on making the most efficient use of power. Obviously, the more power the better.

Weight training has produced such remarkable results in so many sports, including shot-putting, that this method is often regarded with awe, as if it were a magical and mysterious activity. It isn't. Weight training is an exercise system. There are lots of ways to exercise, but the special advantage of weight training is that it provides more control than other exercise methods. In weight training you can control both the muscles that are emphasized and the amounts of resistance offered to these muscles. In this book we are directly concerned with shot-putting and cannot go into the topic of weight training in a detailed way, but the more comprehensive your understanding of weight training, the more you will profit from it.

In approaching weight training, you should give safety precautions first priority. Methods of avoiding injury should be learned right away and established as habit. Weight training can and should be a very safe activity.

Many weight-training exercises have been developed, but it won't take you long to get familiar with them. Work with very light weights until you get used to the different exercises. Later on, there will be time to pile on the weight.

The individual exercises are the elements from which programs are constructed. An almost infinite variety of programs is possible. The basic variables in program construction are the exercises selected, the number of repetitions, and the number of sets. Your program is built to accomplish your purpose. There are two extreme orientations or emphases. Your program can be primarily aimed at building either endurance or strength. Or, of course, you can aim for some combination of the two.

As a shot-putter you know there will be two important aspects of your weight-training program. First, you know that eventually you will be lifting fairly heavy weights. Your emphasis will be on poundage rather than repetitions. Putting the shot requires power more than endurance. So you will want to set up a program directed toward the acquisition of great strength.

Second, experience suggests the most valuable basic exercises for the shot-putter are squats and presses. Presses include the standing or military press, bench press, and incline press. These are the "bread and butter" exercises of nearly all great shot-putters. These exercises form the core of the program. They always remain, even when other exercises are added.

Your first weight-training exercises will be devoted to orientation. This is the time to learn safety precautions and to become familiar with the various exercises. After a preliminary orientation period, you will want to build up muscle tone and general conditioning. That means you will use poundages that allow you to carry out about eight to twelve repetitions and about three or four sets.

Eventually you will reduce the number of repetitions and increase the poundages. There are various ways of setting up programs. Most shot-putters think the so-called ladder method has been of great benefit. An example of the "ladder" would be as follows: You start by bench pressing poundage that just allows you to make five reps. You then add weight until you can just manage four reps. And so it goes until you have added poundage that you can lift just once. You can keep going and work down the other side of the ladder, which means that you keep reducing poundage until you are back where you started at five repetitions. However, at the present time most shot-putters use only the "up" portion of the ladder.

The critical point about weight training is that it should be progressive. That is, as the muscles get used to handling certain poundages, it is time to increase the weight and thus give the body a new level of poundage to adjust to. Experience suggests that the body adjusts best if lifting is carried out about every other day, which means, of course, a day of relative rest after each session.

When weight training was first recognized as a valuable preparation for effective shot-putting, lifting was strictly a preseason activity. Now weight training extends right through the competitive season, although its intensity is usually somewhat reduced. Both the poundage and the number of lifting days are less. For example, the preseason program might be lifting on Mondays, Wednesdays, and Fridays. When the meets start, poundage is reduced, and lifting on Fridays is eliminated.

Running. Running is a vital part of your conditioning program. There should seldom be a practice day when you don't do some running. You include two types of running workouts—distance and speed. Since the shot-putter's performance depends upon a powerful explosion, it may seem strange he should be concerned with the slower tempo of distance running. But this type of running has remarkable health benefits, especially for the heart and lungs. Shot-putters have been taking to the cross country courses, where they jog or run.

Sprinters are getting used to the sight of shot-putters working alongside them. At first, the weight men were regarded with curiosity, but more and more of them are beginning to make sprint relay teams. And, of course, their shot-putting is benefiting from this speed work.

Although much of your practice time should be spent in actual putting, so that you can keep improving your technique, weight training and running are needed to develop strength, speed, and conditioning.

Standing Put

In this section we will be talking about getting started on actual shot-putting. When we talk about the "standing put," we mean the action that takes place at the front of the circle. It involves acquiring a sound power position and then making the most effective use of this position.

Handhold. The shot has to be held, so the handhold is a good starting place for discussion. You should feel the center of the shot against the base of your fingers. Let your fingers spread easily and comfortably. The grip is loose. There is no effort to squeeze the shot. The three middle fingers are going to supply propulsion. Neither the thumb nor the little finger can contribute much to the push. For this reason the thumb and little finger are best used to steady the shot in place.

The handhold is easy to learn. You just have to watch for two common mistakes. The shot might be held either too low or too high. You can quickly see how ineffective a very low grip would be. If the shot were to be held against the palm of the hand, the fingers could not make a contribution to shot velocity. A very high grip has no value and is inevitably harmful. Some years ago in the belief that more "finger snap" could be obtained, shot-putters were often taught to perch the shot well up toward the fingertips. This high handhold caused unnecessary muscle tension and resulted in many sprained fingers.

The shot is tucked easily and naturally against the neck. The rules don't require that the shot be in contact with the neck. They specify only that the shot cannot be held behind the shoulder. From time to time athletes and coaches have experimented with various off-the-neck carries. The theory was that with the shot held farther back the length of the drive could be increased. Such carries never worked out well. Holding the shot against the neck is needed for control, stability, and alignment.

Right arm position. With the shot held against the neck, the putting arm is, of course, bent. Although the amount of bend is automatically determined, there still remains much to be done. Effective arm position does not come naturally, and acquiring it is usually a tantalizing task. Arm position should receive a great deal of early attention. The arm has a tendency to drift out of position, so constant checking is needed.

The correct position of the putting arm is easy to describe. If you were to draw a straight line from the left shoulder to the right shoulder, a continuation of this straight line would extend to the right elbow. The putting arm can be regarded as an extension of the shoulders. The putting arm remains in alignment with the shoulders until delivery is begun.

Dropping the right elbow is a natural, and therefore a tenacious, error. If you are supporting a weight in your hand, it's more easily done when your elbow is directly under the weight. Effective putting requires that the elbow be high enough to be in alignment with the shoulders. As mentioned, because the error of lowering the right elbow comes from a natural tendency, its correction is going to take full and early attention.

The other error of nonalignment is letting the elbow move forward. This is a type of error that shows up in nearly all motor learning. It's called an "error of anticipation." That means looking ahead too far and anticipating the next move too soon. Because we know the job is to drive the shot forward, we tend to swing the elbow forward too soon.

To summarize, the elbow of the putting arm should be in alignment with the shoulders in two planes—the vertical plane and the horizontal plane. Nonalignment is a natural error. So early in the game try to build the habit of keeping the elbow both high and back.

Left arm position. The left arm is bent, loose, and relaxed with the hand toward the rear of the circle. The left hand should be at least as far back as the right hand. The non-putting arm has two important functions. First, it helps keep the shoulders in power position. Second, its action contributes to the drive.

If the left arm is in a favorable position when the delivery is started, it tends to make an efficient contribution to power in a natural and unconscious way. The left arm whips forward and around and in doing so adds to both balance and force. But the action of the left arm should seldom be the object of direct coaching attention. Rather, it should be left to its own timing and movement.

Body position. The greats deliver the shot from a body position that permits long acceleration and a full use of the big muscles of the body. As you look at a photo of Randy Matson reaching his power position at the front of the circle, you'll have an understandable tendency to want to imitate him right away. Of course, you do want to look like Randy, and it is hoped you will. But since the shot-put is an event that places a premium on natural movement, it is best to reach an effective power position by comfortable and smooth stages. So our process of learning to make a long and powerful drive of the shot should be simple, natural, and easily understood.

Your first putting stance should stress comfort. Your feet are lined up in the approximate direction you expect the shot to go. A line drawn from your right foot to your left would point to about the landing spot for the shot. Your knees should be bent slightly. Feel loose and relaxed. Stand straight and naturally. Don't bend forward from the waist or try to crouch. If you think of supporting a weight on your shoulders, you'll probably hit the right body position.

A feeling of comfort and naturalness is very important. Checkpoints are your head, your legs, and your trunk. The head is in a natural position with no thought of aiming the shot. Line of vision is parallel to the ground. Legs are slightly flexed and should feel springy. The trunk is comfortably erect. It's a good idea to try this position first without the shot in your hand.

When you do pick up the shot, place it at the base of your fingers. Right elbow is high and back. The left arm is bent and relaxed. The head assumes a natural position in alignment with the body. That means your line of vision is always at right angles to the line of your shoulders. Later on in your progress when the shoulders are cocked, the relative positions of your head and shoulders will remain the same.

Make your initial stance as good as you can, but don't feel that this position has to be perfect before you actually start putting the shot. Don't worry too much about errors. Expect to make many of them. Just drive the shot forward, and go retrieve it to put it again. Get a measuring tape, and put out some markers. It's fun to watch your progress.

Puts should be made without too much delay. That is, you shouldn't spend a lot of time holding your stance, worrying about whether your position is right. Remaining in position a long time makes for stiffness and loss of rhythm. When you feel it necessary to spend considerable time checking your putting position, do so without the shot. Try to get the best possible image and muscle feel for the position you would like. Think clearly, but when you actually pick up the shot, don't spend a lot of time holding it before you put. Move decisively.

Early puts. Your first puts should be low. Later on, you will want to get more height on your puts, but this height will result correctly, easily, and naturally from the use of the leg muscles and the muscles of the trunk. If you try directly for shot height during the early stages, you can develop errors that will plague you later.

A theme that you've been hearing and will hear again is that much of the effective action of the shot-put is natural. When you watch a great shot-putter you are struck by the utter simplicity and naturalness of his delivery. This suggests an important general principle. In learning to put the shot, the natural, almost instinctive, movements of the athlete should be preserved. For example, in delivering the shot the fairly talented beginner tends to make a full and high sweep of the right shoulder pretty much as do the champs. It would be a mistake to tamper with this natural action. Of course, learning does have to take place. Not all aspects of technique are completely natural. But learning should emphasize a framework in which many of the athlete's natural movements can be preserved and used effectively.

We keep emphasizing that much of shot-put movement is natural and should be left to your own "muscle feel." What does this view mean to you in terms of your learning approach? In general, it means that your emphasis should be on basics. To the extent that you can, you avoid details and, instead, concentrate on the fundamentals, including the whys. By working on these fundamentals you establish a framework that allows your natural movements to express themselves. This approach is useful right away. In making your first standing puts think mostly of feeling solid and balanced. Think of your legs as springy and comfortably placed. Think of your arm drive as being straight and simple.

Where you are now. You've made a start and perhaps established a sound base for future progress. You've learned the handhold. You have been trying to keep your flexed putting arm in alignment with your shoulders. You've been getting used to a comfortable, erect body position, a position from which you feel you could support a weight on your shoulders. And you have gained a certain amount of familiarity with the event.

After this period of working on some fundamentals and getting an orientation that makes you feel more comfortable with the shot-put, you are ready to go on to the next task. And the next task is to increase the length of drive on the shot and to bring the big muscles of the body into greater use.

You already know that the distance the shot will travel depends primarily on its velocity at the moment of release. The longer you can drive the shot, the faster you can get it going—and the farther it will go. You increase the length of the drive on the shot in two ways. First, you start the drive earlier or farther back toward the rear of the circle. Second, you lengthen the forward part of the drive by making a follow-through. Both of these ways of increasing the length of drive should get intensive practice attention. It's best, however, to start by increasing the first part of the drive.

Getting farther back. In an early part of this book are action sequences of the greats. In this section the power positions are reproduced, the positions reached at completion of the glide across the circle. The pictures are worth studying, because they bring a clear image of what a really effective power position looks like. The basic point to note is that each athlete is back in a position that permits a long acceleration of the shot. Of the three greats Randy Matson appears to be the farthest back toward the rear of the circle.

Although the "back" position is the most obvious and important feature shown by the pictures, there are other vital and related points to observe. In each case notice: (1) the bend of the right leg; (2) the right foot pointing partially toward the rear; (3) the "closed" position of the shoulders; and (4) the head position with vision toward the rear. These points are all critical to the achievement of an effective power position, and they help make the best use of this position. As you work on your power position, you will concentrate on each of these points.

Another reminder about naturalness of action and comfort. As you work to acquire a good power position, move with rhythm and ease. You should never feel off-balance or strained. And no movement or position should feel artificial.

It's a good idea to begin your first approach to the power position by way of "dummy" drills or "dry runs." This means going through the motions without the shot. In this way you are freer to concentrate on the movements you are trying to master.

The dummy drills are begun as follows: Stand comfortably erect with your feet fairly close together. Your line of vision should be at about right angles to the direction in which the shot would be put. Even if you don't actually have a shot in your hand, your arms assume the same positions they would if the shot were present. Relaxation, comfort, and balance are the main considerations. Don't hold the position too long. Try it. Walk away. Then go back to the starting position again.

A quick review of the starting position for the standing put: you are erect, comfortable, and your feet are close together. The next move is to swing back into a power position, a position that might resemble those of the champions we've been looking at in this section.

Start by swinging your body weight both forward and around to your left. This preliminary action starts an easy and rhythmic motion and puts your body weight over your left foot. When you have rotated slightly to your left and centered your weight over your left leg, the right leg is free to move. Now, picking up the rhythm, reverse the direction of body rotation so that you are now turning to your right. At the same time, pick up your right foot and move it smoothly backward toward the center of the circle. Let your body weight move backward so that it is entirely supported over the right leg.

Try this action again and again. Start by standing erect. Feet are placed together. You rotate partially to your left. Body weight shifts forward over the left leg. Picking up the rhythm of the movement, reverse your body rotation so that the turning is now toward your right, and, at the same time, the right foot is swung toward the rear. Your body rotates and moves backward so that your weight is balanced over the right leg.

When you are first practicing the swing back into power position, hold the position long enough to check yourself. Later on you will bounce right out of this position and into the drive of the shot. But in the beginning it's best to stop and make sure you are reaching an effective power position. A solid power position is all-important to your future progress. Check the following points:

(1) Right foot. Is it back far enough? A distance from the left foot of about 3 to 3½ feet is about correct. Is the right toe pointed partially toward the rear? This foot position is important to both comfort and drive.

(2) Is your right leg bent? By bending the leg you improve your balance. And a bent right leg is needed for power.

(3) Shoulders. Are they "closed"? A line drawn between the shoulders should be approximately at right angles to the intended direction of shot flight.

(4) Head position. Has your head rotated smoothly with your body so

that your vision is toward the rear? Head position is important in establishing a powerful driving position.

(5) Arm positions. Is your right elbow in alignment with your shoulders on both planes? Is your left arm bent and toward the rear?

We've been emphasizing the checking of the power position because of its great importance. A correct power position is really the basic key to great performance. Early in your career this position rates a lot of attention. But even when you become a champ, you will still check on your power position.

Thus far you have been working on a swing back to power position and then holding this position to give you more time to check on the various points of form. There comes a time, however, when you swing into power position and bounce right out into a forward drive and lift. In actual putting, the power position should not be held. It's a position you go through rather than hold. If the position were held, the action would tend to be artificial and stilted. Continuity and rhythm are always important to athletic performance.

After a certain amount of dummy work, you carry out the movements with a shot. You swing back into power position and from this power position you drive the shot forward. Earlier we talked about the weight of the shot. In order to carry out the technique correctly and smoothly the shot must feel light to you. A "heavy" shot would interfere with your ability to perform. That's why it's useful to start with a light shot and increase the weight of the shot only as you become stronger.

How is the shot driven from the power position? If you wanted to you could, through the use of slow-motion film, make a fairly precise analysis of the body positions, the muscles involved, and the sequence of actions. Carrying out such an analysis might be enlightening for the athletic coach or the graduate student in physical education. But for the athlete a detailed preoccupation with body action tends to cause artificial and self-conscious movement in an event that places a great premium on natural movement.

When you reach a sound power position, the movements tend to trigger themselves naturally. Action takes place around all three axes of the body, and these movements blend into each other. There is a blending of lifting, twisting, and forward drive. All muscles play a part. Reach a good power position, and then your body has a chance to react effectively. Your own "feel" for applying power is the best first guide to delivery technique. This guide may not be foolproof in that some errors may still remain, but such an approach is a good starting point. The errors that do remain will need correction and special attention, but there may be few of them.

Driving farther forward. The longer the drive, the more you can speed up the shot and the farther it will go. You started from an erect body position. You've then been working to increase the length of the first part of the drive by obtaining a "back" position. The next step is to increase the length of the forward portion of the drive.

You naturally want to keep driving the shot as far as the "law allows." In other words you want to stay with the shot as long as you can and still not foul. Hence, the reverse becomes important. As the word suggests, the reverse amounts to a reversing of the feet. At the last moment of shot delivery the left leg is supplying its final drive. The right leg, having completed its drive, continues forward in a circular path. As the left leg finishes its drive, it moves toward the rear. The right foot lands in about the same position that had been occupied by the left foot.

A description of the reverse makes this fairly simple action sound complicated. You can think of the reverse as a simple switching of the feet. When you exchange the positions of your feet, you'll simply find it easier and more natural to let your left foot remain in the air.

The reverse lets you continue forward drive and follow-through as far as possible and still remain in the circle. Without making a reverse you just could not get the best follow-through. When you realize that you want your right hand to go as far forward as possible and still make a fair put, you will understand an important advantage of the reverse.

When you complete the reverse and land on the right leg, you let the leg bend and relax. By bending the right leg you accomplish two objectives. First, it's easier to keep your balance over a bent leg. Second, by bending your leg you lower your body's center of gravity and in this way increase your stability. You become more solid and are in less danger of falling out of the circle.

With the body weight centered over your right leg, the left leg is pointed directly toward the rear. It is as far back as possible. The reason is simple. The leg is a heavy part of your body, and bringing it back as far as possible helps to keep the body's center of gravity back. That means that you can reach farther forward and still retain balance.

Ideally, after delivery of the shot the right shoulder and arm should continue past the median line. What do we mean by this? Picture a line from you to where the shot lands. A full and natural reverse and follow-through would bring your right shoulder and right arm slightly to the left of such a line. The reason is as follows. The shot-put had always been looked upon as a linear event—that is, with the drive in a straight line. But with weight training bringing about greatly increased strength a partial rotary or centrifugal motion became effective. The "closed" position of the shoulders in the power position represents something of a winding. If you wind up and then unwind, as you should if you're strong enough, then the natural and effective follow-through is with the right shoulder and right arm past the median line. In other words, since the drive is partially round, the follow-through should also be partially round. Try to get this "round" follow-through, but if you don't learn it right away, there's no reason to be discouraged. A number of world record holders failed to carry it out well. Randy Matson is one of the few greats who can easily and naturally finish past the median line.

Do some dummy work with the reverse and follow-through. It helps you to get the feel of this action. Be conscious of the forward stretch of the right hand, the bend of the right knee, and the backward position of the left leg. Make this pattern as automatic as possible. This practice will surely pay off. You will get a longer drive on the shot, and you will save many puts that would otherwise be fouls.

Brief review. We've been working on the standing put. We started with a comfortably erect stance. Particular attention was paid to arm position. When holding the shot against the neck, the upper arm can be viewed as an extension of the shoulders. Alignment is important.

We emphasized that in making early puts there should be a natural arm movement with no effort to get height on the shot. Our next step was to increase the length of the drive on the shot and to make greater use of the big muscles of the body. There are two ways of increasing the length of drive and thereby increasing the acceleration of the shot. First, you work for a "back" position in which your trunk is inclined to the rear and your body weight is balanced over a bent right leg. Shoulders are "closed." This is the all-important power position. Second, you work to increase the forward part of your drive. You learn a full follow-through and a reverse.

When the standing put is in reasonably good shape, it's time to add momentum to it. That's our next step.

4. Handhold is easy to learn. Center of the shot is against the base of the fingers. The fingers are spread easily. Thumb and little finger help steady the shot in place. The shot is tucked against the neck.

4a

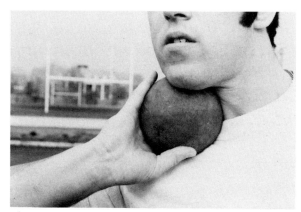

4b

4c

4d

5. Elbow is back and high. Ideally, the upper arm is in line with the shoulders in two planes.

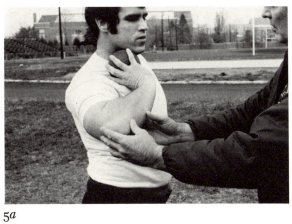

5*a*

5*b*

6. The left arm helps establish power position and contributes to the drive.

7. Early puts are made from a comfortable and erect position. There is no effort to obtain shot height.

7a

7b

8. Power positions of the all-time greats.

8a

8b

9. Swinging to the back position. Body weight is over the bent right leg.

8c

10. The reverse makes for a longer follow-through. You can reach farther forward from your right foot.

10*a*

10*b*

11. The reverse can first be seen as a simple switching of the feet.

12. After the feet are changed, the left leg remains in the air.

13. Checking out features of the follow-through. A bent right leg and the arm past the median line.

Across the Circle

The glide across the circle has two simple purposes—to get you into power position and to do so with momentum. The two tests of your glide, then, are as follows: Do you finish the glide in a solid power position? Do you have momentum when you reach position?

Both speed and position are important. Without momentum the glide would have no value, because for practical purposes you would simply have a standing put. If the glide fails to produce a good power position, it may actually be harmful and detract from distance. There would be only a short drive, and very little use could be made of the big muscles. So both factors are needed—speed and drive.

Where do you put your emphasis in practice sessions? On position! The reason for concentration on position is simple. Speed has a way of creeping up on you. Your natural speed and the speed otherwise developed will tend to be asserted without much conscious effort. But not so with position. The power position is elusive. It is not easily attained. Getting into a solid power position will be the objective of much of your practice time. It's going to take a lot of concentration, repetition, and intelligent effort. Your mental image of the power position and your muscle feel for it should be clearly established as soon as possible. And this image and feel should become increasingly vivid as you practice.

Dummy runs. While being introduced to the standing put, you probably found it valuable to do your first work without the shot. You should find it equally useful to start learning the glide across the circle by means of dry runs. In the early stages the presence of the shot tends to be somewhat inhibiting and distracting. Without the shot you are freer to concentrate on the movements you want to learn. It's not exactly exciting to go through the motions of the shot-put without making an actual put. But if you can be patient the dummy runs will really speed up learning. If, however, you do start with a shot in your hand (a light one), the learning procedure is about the same.

At the rear of the circle. In a complete put everything starts at the rear of the circle. You have 7 feet in which to accelerate the shot. About half of the circle is used to build up momentum and reach a power position. The forward half of the circle is used for the final drive, an action similar to the standing put you've been working on.

The glide across the circle is intended to provide both acceleration and a solid power position. In terms of mechanics these two goals are somewhat opposed to each other. You have to seek the best compromise. Let's see what this means. If sheer speed were your only goal, you would adopt a pattern similar to that used by a sprinter. The sprinter is in the best position to accelerate when the axis of his body is tilted forward. The speed of the glide can indeed be increased by inclining your body toward the front of the circle, but, although you'd be faster, you would not be able to reach an effective power position. On the other hand, if you were to start with your body inclined toward the rear of the circle, you might ensure position, but you could not develop much momentum. The best glide is the one that gives you the right combination of speed and position. As you will see, the O'Brien Technique solves the problem of speed versus position very nicely.

The best position at the back of the circle is one of comfort and balance. Your right foot is pointed directly to the rear with the toes near the rim of the circle. Your shoulders are "closed"—that is, the direction of the shoulders is at about a right angle to the intended direction of shot flight. Vision is focused on a spot on the ground about 5 yards to the rear. Body is fairly erect with only a slight "back" inclination of the trunk. The front of the left foot can be in contact with the ground to supply additional stability.

In understanding and describing the glide, we look at the actions of the *legs* and the *trunk*. These actions are closely interrelated. They depend on each other to make for a coordinated movement across the circle and into position. When we talk about what the left leg does, the action of the right leg and what happens to the trunk, we have to keep in mind that all of these movements are parts of an overall pattern. No single action is understandable without reference to the whole. So when we describe the movement of one part of the body, it is somewhat artificial and done only to make description easier. With that caution let's look at the individual actions.

Legs. The left leg moves a little like a pendulum. It moves in only one plane—back and forth in a plane directly across the circle. When you are ready to start the glide, the left leg is swung forward and upward, then downward. As the left foot touches or nears the ground, the left leg without breaking rhythm again starts upward and forward. It continues to move forward and up until it strikes its contact spot at the front of the circle.

As the left leg swings forward, the sole of the foot is toward the front of the circle. Movement is rhythmic and free. The word "free" is significant. You swing the left leg forward and upward easily and smoothly without an attempt to force either its direction or height. Two more things have to be done, but they tend to take care of themselves. The left foot has to turn so that the toes are pointing partially forward, and the foot has to land at the right time. Both of these actions and their timings should occur naturally. They should never be forced. Although it sounds extreme, a practical approach is to swing the left leg forward and up and then almost forget about it.

The job of the right leg is to drive the body forward—to develop momentum. It's a very powerful action. The right leg operates in precise but natural coordination with the action of the left leg. At the start your right leg is only slightly flexed. It stays about the same as your left leg makes its preliminary swing. Now, as the left leg lowers, your right knee bends. The right leg drive starts as the left leg moves forward and upward.

The timing between left and right leg action is highly important. Let's look again at the coordination between the two legs. At the rear of the circle, your body weight is comfortably balanced over a fairly straight right leg. The feet are close together with the left toe in contact with the ground to increase comfort and stability. When you feel ready, you make a preliminary swing of your left leg which brings it forward and upward. As your left leg comes backward again, your right leg bends. The left leg completes its downward swing and immediately starts forward and up. Just as the left leg nears its full forward and up position, the right leg drives. If you permit your left leg to swing freely in alignment with the direction you intend to move, you quickly develop a feel for the timing of the right leg drive.

The action across the circle is rhythmic, continuous, and fully committed. Once you decide that you are ready to go, there should be no pauses, no hesitations, and no indecision. You should feel fully committed to a rhythmic pattern that takes you across the circle and results in a completed put.

In crossing the circle the body's center of gravity remains low. Some years ago, the movement across the circle was called the "hop," and a hop it was. There was a highly inefficient up and down action. The lift of the body interfered with both continuity and position. It is now clear that the body's center of gravity should stay low until the power position is reached. In driving across the circle the right foot barely leaves the ground. In fact, the right foot scrapes along the ground for the first part of its drive. Drive is powerful and low.

The right leg is the source of speed and power across the circle. But as soon as the right leg becomes fully extended, its initial contribution is finished. The right leg has contributed all it can to forward power. But the right leg also has a second and important function. It must contribute to the final drive. Hence, the right leg must recover quickly and be in position for its next effort. In other words, the right leg has two drives to make. Its first drive moves you across the circle from the starting position to a power position. Its second drive directly powers the shot. After the right leg completes its first drive, it is straight or extended. It has to be bent again before it can be ready for its second drive. There is very little time to recover the right leg—that is, to take it from a straight position to a bent position. The movement is a skilled one that requires practice. Although the action is fast, it is carried out with rhythm.

You will note from the photos that, during the movement of the right leg, the right foot turns slightly. At the start the toe is pointed directly backward. On landing it is only partially so. You don't have to practice this movement, because it comes about naturally.

Trunk. For good performance the big muscles of the trunk must strike a heavy blow and give impetus to the shot. But before the trunk can contribute it must be inclined toward the rear. It must be in a "back" position. A power position in which the trunk is laid back is the hallmark of the fine performer. Much of your practice effort will be concerned with getting your back to the rear and ready to strike.

Let's take a look at the trunk position from the start through to power position. When you take your initial stance at the rear of the circle, your trunk is fairly upright. Your trunk is erect so that your body can be balanced. Your trunk can incline toward the rear only when it can do so and still retain body balance. Now we have to see how we can get a back position of the trunk and still keep balance.

The key to getting back position of the trunk while maintaining body balance lies in the action of the left leg. As the left leg moves forward it moves the center of gravity forward. This means that there can be a compensating action of the trunk toward the rear. In a sense the two actions, left leg forward and the trunk inclined toward the rear, cancel each other's effect on the center of gravity. Hence, the center of gravity tends to remain over the right leg, and balance is maintained.

All parts of the body are coordinated, but the coordination between trunk inclination to the rear and the left leg action is particularly clear and interesting. After the left leg's preliminary swing, it should not come all the way back to its starting place, but only partially back. The left leg must remain at least partly forward to compensate for the inclined position of the trunk. Balance must be maintained.

At the start of the right leg drive the great shot-putters show an extreme back position of the trunk. The trunk is almost parallel to the ground. When power position is reached, the trunk is still well back, but it usually rises somewhat. By beginning to move slightly toward the erect position a kind of "running start" is created.

Closed position. The closed position of the upper body is set up at the very start and is maintained right into power position. Vision is fixed toward the rear. The shoulders are aligned at about right angles to the front of the circle. It takes patience and practice to hold this closed upper body position as you move across the circle. But the closed position is needed to help supply the whip that makes the shot go.

Distance of the glide. How far should the glide take you? The power position is most effective when the right foot lands at about the center of the circle. The distance that the right leg will drive you forward during the glide depends on two things—the power of the drive and the height attained by your body's center of gravity. We want the power of the drive without too much distance. If you allow your body to rise, even a mild drive of the right leg could drive you too far forward and crowd you against the front of the circle. The answer is to keep your body low during movement across the circle. In this way you can drive forward as hard as possible and still not have your right foot move too close to the front of the circle. In brief, you get the correct distance of the right foot during the glide not by trying to place it in a specific spot, but by keeping a low center of gravity.

In this section we've been concerned with movement across the circle. As you work out, you will get much more from your efforts if your notions about the glide are clear. There are details, but all of them should make sense to you within the over-all goal of the movement across the circle. The only goal of the glide is to get you into position with momentum. There is no other. Everything that is done must in some way contribute to either position or speed.

14. Coach demonstrates correct position, in which the body is fairly erect.

15. Balance will produce a solid position over the right leg.

16. Relation between "back" position of trunk and use of left leg. Parry O'Brien starts in erect position and inclines backward only when left leg is forward to supply balance.

16*b*

16*c*

16*d*

16*e*

16*f*

16*g*

16*h*

Daily Practice

Many fine athletes have gone the route that you are now taking. Obviously, it is highly useful for you to benefit from their experience. It's helpful to know what they have run into along the way. There are nagging errors common to all, and there are valuable insights, views, and procedures. In your daily practice sessions you are bound to be confronted by just about the same problems and situations that the greats encountered.

Your approach to achievement is really two-pronged. Your strength and conditioning program is basic. To perform well you must be both strong and in good shape. Strength and technique are related, because technique really amounts to the efficiency with which power is applied. Also, you must be strong to carry out certain techniques.

The more clearly you understand your event, the faster and surer your progress will be. An over-all orientation is important in guiding your day-to-day activities. Every aspect of shot-put form ought to make sense to you. Nothing should be learned or carried out blindly. You ought to know the why of everything you do.

Again, your understanding of the event will be your biggest asset. As we talk about some specifics, fit them into the over-all picture.

Warming up. One important difference between the average performer and the great performer is that the latter always insists on a thorough warm-up. The average athlete often tends to regard his warm-up as an unimportant preliminary action—perhaps a whim of the coach or a trivial ritual to be done quickly. In contrast, the experienced athlete has found that the warm-up is an essential and valuable part of his workout pattern. He knows that his warm-up can never be slighted or neglected.

There are many different ways of warming up, but all of them include various combinations of jogging, striding, and calisthenics. You really warm up twice. You have a general warm-up appropriate for almost any athletic event, and you have another warm-up that is specific for the shot-put.

The main purposes of the warm-up are to make the muscles more efficient and to reduce the chances of injury. The subjective feelings of an experienced athlete are usually reliable. He generally knows when the blood is saturating his muscles and the muscles are truly loose. But the beginner will be better off if he works out a definite warm-up routine. It's best to adhere to a schedule that specifies the exact amounts of jogging, striding, and calisthenics—just to make sure.

When you finish your general warm-up and reach the shot-put circle, your second warm-up begins. This, however, is a simple one. You start with very easy puts and then gradually build up the effort. The first puts are usually taken from the standing position.

In your practice sessions you can control the conditions under which you warm up. This may not be so before formal competition. At a large meet there are many competitors, and the circle is in great demand. You may not be able to get in many puts before the competition starts. For this reason you may have to be flexible and use some ingenuity. Place greater reliance on calisthenics and dummy runs.

The toeboard. When should you start using a toeboard? Almost any time you want to, but it does seem best to have some orientation to your event before making an adjustment to the presence of the board. In the beginning stages you are freer to perform without the board, and your concentration on what you are learning tends to be better. It is much easier to work with the board after you become a little used to the shot-put. In general, it seems a good idea to introduce the board when your complete form takes up about 7 feet of space. If you are faced with immediate competition you may have to start using the toeboard sooner.

In the very beginning the presence of the toeboard may be somewhat distracting and inhibiting, but you'll soon get used to it. You will, in fact, get so used to the toeboard that you will become uncomfortable without it.

Power position. We've talked a lot about power position. We should, because it's that important. The idea of a good power position seems simple enough. In essence you want to be "back" when you finish the glide across the circle so that you can get a long drive on the shot, a drive that is not only long but makes efficient use of the big muscles of the body. The main features to keep checking are: legs in alignment with the direction of shot flight, body weight balanced over a bent right leg, trunk inclined toward the rear of the circle, and a closed position of the shoulders.

Although an understanding of the power position is a vital first step in learning, much daily work remains to be done. Even the talented beginner finds that his right foot drifts far to the right and that his left foot tends to move left to the "bucket." His body weight is forward over the left leg, and the shoulders are open. The head is usually turned forward. The power position is elusive.

The error of a poor power position is frustrating and tenacious. It doesn't do much good to work directly on details. For example, you might be aware that your left foot lands too far over in the "bucket." You know that this position makes a strong contrast to that of Randy Matson's left foot, which is straight down the center of the circle. It is natural enough to think that you can directly imitate Randy's excellent left foot placement. But you can't. Direct efforts just don't work. It has to be done the way Randy did it. That means a clear and very deep understanding of position and what it does for power. When such an understanding becomes conviction, then the left foot tends to land in the right spot.

Every athletic event requires concentration, and it seems that most events require sudden shifts in concentration or perception. In the shot-put, as you cross the circle, you should be concentrating on position. The split second that effective power position is assured, you should switch your concentration to explosion or delivery. The quick shift in perception is not easy. It's a tough psychological trick, but it does produce results.

To sum up what we've been talking about. An effective power position is absolutely essential to top performance. This position is not easy to acquire. Most of your competitors will not master it. The way to acquire a good power position is not by working directly on details but by concentration and by constantly strengthening your mental and muscle images of the position itself. Details may need direct attention at times, but generally these details should be viewed as symptoms rather than objects of direct coaching attack.

Delivery of the shot. The final impetus given to the shot is naturally of great importance. The delivery is an all-out effort with every muscle of the body playing a part in producing maximum distance. There are a number of practical points to be taken into account.

First, the power position is the base for a good delivery. Without a sound power position, there is no possibility of an effective delivery. Conversely, if the power position is solid, a powerful and full delivery is almost assured. At the very least, a good chance for an effective delivery is there.

Second, the only effective delivery is a natural one. If you give the delivery more attention than it needs, you are likely to produce artificial action and thus cut down on distance.

Third, the delivery action must be continuous. Once you start the action, you go all the way—win, lose, or draw. When you pull the trigger, you can't shoot a bullet a little bit at a time. There has to be full commitment. When the delivery starts, it's not the time to stop to think things over.

What do these points mean for your daily practice sessions? Realizing that your delivery must be as natural as possible, you don't spend excessive practice time in masterminding it. You treat the delivery as a full and continuous unit. It is no accident that the poor shot-putters can usually describe in detail the movements of their deliveries, whereas the greats are often vague and inaccurate in this area.

You probably won't be able to avoid hearing the word "snap." Well-wishers may urge you to work on snap to make the shot "really go." In a well-executed put there is a kind of snap, but the snap amounts to the wrist and fingers adding to the final acceleration at a point when the shot should be moving pretty fast anyway. This kind of snap is a culmination of a natural movement. In contrast, direct efforts to snap the shot are harmful in that they both interfere with natural delivery movement and produce sprained fingers.

The start at the rear of the circle. When you move across the circle you do want to have a back position of the trunk. But timing is important. The shot-putter usually tries to assume this position as soon as he takes his starting stance. As a result he is off balance and not ready to drive forward. All of his weight goes over his right toes. The right heel is off the ground. His leg trembles, and he feels uncomfortable and unstable.

The solution to this common problem is to assume a starting position with the body fairly erect. Because there is then body balance over the right leg, the right foot feels in solid contact with the ground. Now, as the left leg is swung forward, the trunk is inclined toward the rear. The two movements, of the left leg and the trunk, compensate each other. As a result, body balance remains over the right leg, and the right foot remains stable.

In short, an unstable and therefore ineffective starting position at the rear of the circle is caused by trying to assume a back position too early. The back position of the trunk has to be timed with the forward swing of the left leg.

Distance across the circle. A common error is to move too far forward during the glide. The feet get bunched in the front of the circle, and there is neither space nor position for an effective delivery. The error of landing with the right foot too far forward is caused by lifting the body's center of gravity as the glide starts. You can drive as hard as you want and still place the right foot near the center of the circle—if you drive forward instead of upward.

Left leg action. Nearly all beginners and a lot of pretty good shot-putters have persistent difficulty in making correct use of the left leg as they cross the circle. The movement looks artificial and stilted, and the action of the left leg becomes inefficient in a number of ways. This poor action derives from an attempt to place the leg instead of swinging it. The key is to swing —do not place. The champ swings the left leg fully and freely. He does this with confidence. The leg is swung forward and upward without anxiety about where and when it is going to land. In contrast, the beginner cautiously places his left leg in a kind of probing motion. A tip-off is foot position at the start of the swing. The champ's left leg swing starts with the sole of the foot toward the front of the circle. The beginner tends to rotate the leg and point his toe forward.

Correct left leg action is, of course, a critical aspect of shot-put form, primarily because of its influence on power position. Faulty left leg action can interfere both with getting back and with correct alignment.

Curiously, one error in the use of the left leg seems to come about deliberately. Many shot-putters have the notion that the left leg should be forced or slammed down quickly at the front of the circle. The idea expressed is that this direct attempt to put the left foot in quick contact with the circle will force a good power position. This effort is harmful. It does not ensure power position, and it interferes with timing and continuity.

The real basis for good power position is balance over the right leg. Depend on balance over the right leg for your position. Let the left leg time itself. The legs should not be forced to land simultaneously. Landing is on the right leg followed by the left.

Using the power position. Getting into the power position is a skilled act. When you can do it, you are well on your way to real achievement. But making full use of the power position is also a skilled act. When the power position is first acquired, it is often "given away." The big muscles of the body are in position to strike, but they don't. There tends to be a drifting forward before the putting action is under way.

There is then usually a lapse between acquiring the ability to reach a good power position and acquiring the ability to make use of this position. For a time the shot-putter looks close to fine performance but still doesn't quite make it. Then there comes a time when he does make it. It seems to happen suddenly, and there is a dramatic improvement in performance. The athlete one day gets a "click" feeling. He feels his legs and back lifting the shot, and the shot sails several feet beyond his old record. If you work on position, sooner or later you will make use of your position. But the task is to make it sooner. There is probably no set formula, but there is the case of one fine athlete who improved four feet in a single day by suddenly making use of his power position. He said that just as he was about to land in power position, he thought of driving the shot high. He felt that thinking of shot height caused him to lift with his back and legs.

Shot height. We've just mentioned the instance of a shot-putter who obtained shot height in the right way—by the use of the big muscles from an effective power position. The best release angle for the shot can be calculated. A projectile moving from ground to ground travels its farthest when released at an angle of 45 degrees. But, of course, the shot is never released at ground level. It's usually released somewhat higher than 7 feet depending upon the athlete's height. In other words the best angle will be less than 45 degrees.

Although it's good to know that the angle of release does affect distance, as a practical matter shot height has to result indirectly. It results from attaining a good power position and the correct use of the big muscles of the body. The trunk and legs supply the needed height.

During your early training you should not give much thought to height. Direct and premature efforts to get height usually result in faulty arm alignment and poor arm action. Height will come when you're ready for it.

Putting hard in practice. If your first concern is learning form, you can and should put hard in practice. As you become more skilled, hard practice puts become more valuable. In the beginning, however, an attempt to go all out will probably produce a wild scramble and very little learning. When your form gets "grooved," hard puts are important to training. At the peak of his career, Parry O'Brien put very hard in practice. He gave the impression that he treated each put as if it were his last chance to win the Olympics. He displayed a remarkable combination of great intensity of effort and concentration on form.

Workout schedules. During the weeks before competition starts, you can work out almost every day. In general, the more days you practice the better. However, most athletes find it psychologically refreshing to take off one day each week.

When the competitive season arrives, your schedule doesn't have to be a delicate and precise matter. There is a wide degree of latitude. But you may want to build up for a competition. Let's assume your meets are on Saturdays. On Monday you work a full session with emphasis on reviewing the previous Saturday's meet and correcting the errors you or your coach perceived. All-out puts should be avoided. Tuesday and Wednesday are days to make a lot of puts with concentration on the points that most need attention. You can't go wrong if you spend much of your time in improving your power position. Thursday should probably be your shortest day. Yet it is an intense day. Warm up thoroughly. Gradually increase the effort of your warm-up puts until you feel ready—just as you would before a competitive put. Then allow yourself as many puts as you can expect in Saturday's competition. "Psych yourself up" so that you can put with the same intensity you would in actual competition. When you have finished the alloted number of puts, stop! Even if you feel that an additional put would solve some problem or give you a better performance, stop! In this way you will bring an "edge" to the meet. Friday should be a day away from the field.

This recommended schedule is not based on scientific findings, but it's astonishing how many fine shot-putters have independently reached a similar schedule. It seems to work well. Try this schedule. You can always change it.

Competition. Be sure you have packed in your canvas bag all the items of personal equipment you will need. Find out in advance the kind of surface from which you will be putting. Chances are the surface will be all-weather, and all you will need are rubber-soled shoes. But, if not, bring along a pair of spikes. Put a towel in your bag in case of rain so that you can dry off the shot and your shoes. Take your own shot along. You may or may not be able to use it in competition, but it can be handy for warming up.

Be on the field early enough to have plenty of time for your warm-up. If the shot-put area is crowded you and a teammate may find a corner of the field where you can get in more warm-up puts than would be possible in the official circle. Even so, try to get in a few full practice puts from the circle to be used in competition.

You will probably be nervous before competition. Be grateful. Nervous energy can work for you. It can add several feet to your best practice performance, if used properly. And that means keeping your poise and concentration.

Be ready when your name is called. That means more than just being in the area. It means being physically and psychologically ready. Learn the throwing order so that you can anticipate when you will be called. When the name several names before yours is called, start moving around and getting ready. Be ready in all ways when you enter the circle.

Do your best. No one can ask for more. As for your coach, he will think his job worthwhile if you try to learn your event in practice and then do your stuff in the meets. As for you, your participation can mean many things, including fun, excitement, frustration, achievement, and perhaps some triumphs. In any case it will be an enriching experience.